Robert Bleakley

AFRICAN MASKS

With 40 color plates

GALLERY BOOKS

An Imprint of W. H. Smith Publishers Inc.
112 Madison Avenue
New York City 10016

The illustration on the cover is of a Bakuba mask, now belonging to the Horniman Museum.

Acknowledgements

THE AUTHOR *and Blacker Calmann Cooper Ltd would like to thank Mr William Fagg, formerly Keeper of the Museum of Mankind and now consultant to Christie Manson and Wood Ltd, for reading the manuscript and advising on it. They would also like to thank Mr John Picton, Deputy Keeper of the Museum of Mankind, Dr John Mack, Assistant Keeper of the Museum of Mankind, Mr John Hewett, Mr John Donne, Miss Felicity Nicholson and the members of the Tribal Art Department of Sotheby Parke Bernet & Co for their advice and help. They are grateful to the museums and collectors who allowed their masks to be reproduced in this book, including Mr Josef Herman (plates 3, 9, 12, 13, 21, 31), Dr Werner Muensterberger (plate 14), Mr Lance Entwistle (plates 18, 20, 23, 25, 30, 34–36) and the Museum of Mankind, London (plates 5–8, 16, 19, 22, 24, 26, 27, 32, 33, 38, 40). Sotheby Parke Bernet & Co provided the transparencies for plates 11 and 29, Robert Harding Associates provided the transparency for the cover subject, and Mr Horst Kolo photographed the masks illustrated in plates 1–9, 12, 13, 15, 16, 18–27, 30–38, 40.*

Published by Gallery Books
An imprint of W.H. Smith Publishers Inc.
112 Madison Avenue
New York, New York 10016

© Blacker Calmann Cooper Ltd, 1978
This book was designed and produced by
Blacker Calmann Cooper Ltd, London

Reprinted 1983

Library of Congress Catalog Card Number: 77-95303

ISBN 0-8317-1075-7

Printed in Spain by Graficromo S.A.

Introduction

THE IMPACT OF AFRICAN ART was first felt in the Western world towards the end of the fifteenth century. Richly carved ivory salt-cellars from the Benin and Sherbro tribes in the region of present-day Nigeria and Sierra Leone were brought to Europe as highly-prized items of trade by Portuguese travellers. It was not, however, until the latter years of the nineteenth century that artifacts from the African continent became readily available to the European collector, and at this time they were considered as nothing more than the handiwork of almost sub-human savages.

European collectors amassed vast collections of tribal artifacts, giving little or no consideration to the aesthetic content of the material; the method of collecting was often thorough almost to the point of obsession. In much the same way as the Impressionists, in particular van Gogh, had been influenced by Japanese wood-block prints brought to Europe as wrapping material and then discarded, many of the most prominent artists of the early twentieth century, particularly Cubists and Expressionists, drew inspiration from tribal art, especially African masks, which passed through the private collections and flea-markets of Europe.

Amongst the artists in whom this influence is readily apparent are Picasso, Matisse, Vlaminck and Derain in Paris, and Nolde and Kirchner in Dresden and Berlin. The utilization of forms and motifs derived from African art by the Cubist/Expressionist artists should not, however, be viewed as an adoption of symbols and forms expressing a sentiment entirely alien to their own. It would be more true to say that the European artists of the period derived inspiration from a sympathetic art which echoed their own developing consciousness.

Although the acceptance of the values of tribal art may appear to be a rapid embracing of a new form of expression, the way had in fact been paved over the preceding fifteen years. For some time artists had been looking back to earlier civilizations and societies, such as those of Egypt, Japan, the Middle East and the early Renaissance, to what they saw as an honesty inherent in the artistic expression of these societies. An attempt was made to cut through the ephemeral extravagances of the late nineteenth century in favour of what was seen as the rejection of irrelevant sophistication by the societies which they flatteringly termed 'primitive'. This movement was, however, in no way similar to the way in which painters several decades earlier had looked back to the Golden Ages of Ancient Greece and the Renaissance. The mood was rather one of optimistic growth, whereas that of the earlier artists was often nihilistic as they viewed all work subsequent to the Golden Ages as being indicative of a process of gradual decline.

African art was especially appealing to the Cubist/Expressionist school of artists in that it differed utterly from the imitation of nature prevalent in Western art since the Renaissance. The African artist created an object which, rather than attempting to mirror nature, was an analogy of natural images. In his carvings, the African artist embodied the vital forces of nature integral to the mystery of the Universe as experienced by man within a tribal context.

One very profound difference does however exist between European 'primitive' painters, especially those of the Expressionist school, and the traditional African artist. The twentieth-century primitive artists have inclined towards images which do not depend on symbolism, whilst the African artist utilized a specific image, given a clearly defined meaning by the tribal tradition. In some cases a strongly derivative element may be apparent in the work of various artists of the Cubist/Expressionist school. In these instances it can be almost certainly assumed that whilst the motifs and forms may bear a close resemblance to each other, the inspiration and understanding of those motifs will be completely different.

Although there are over a thousand tribes in Africa, only a small number produce sculpture and of these, approximately one hundred produce masks. These tribes extend in an arc from Senegal in the north-west to Zambia, Angola and as far south as the Kalahari, with offshoots to the area east of Lake Nyasa. The Negro peoples in these regions can be broadly divided into three groups: peoples of the West African forest and savannah, the Nilotic peoples of the East Sudan, and the Bantu of central, southern and eastern Africa.

Historically, the earliest three-dimensional tribal art known to have been produced in West Africa is a number of terracotta figures from the Nok culture in Nigeria. Through carbon-14 testing, these figures have been shown to date from circa 360 BC and parallel the arrival of the Iron Age in South and West Africa. The growth of civilization in Africa was profoundly affected by stimuli from the civilizations of north Africa and the southernmost tip of Arabia. Immigrants from the North brought with them the benefits of the technically and intellectually advanced civilizations of the Mediterranean region. The cultural influences of these migrations extended west as far as Senegal and south through Lake Chad, along the Benue River to the Niger Delta and as far as the Cameroon Grasslands. Further evidence of these influences having occurred lies in the numerous parallels between the usage of regalia and the incidence of similar motifs in the art of the Black African kingships and the culture of North Africa. It is almost certain that the advanced knowledge of bronze-casting techniques in Black Africa, especially amongst the Benin, may have come through technical knowledge gained from travellers from the north.

It is likely that these invading immigrant groups would have imposed themselves as rulers over the indigenous black tribes. With the passage of time and through the disruption caused by frequent inter-tribal wars, these groups disappeared, being absorbed into the tribal society. Although many of the technological improvements they introduced disappeared with them, agricultural techniques which had a direct application to the Negro way of life were adopted and maintained.

Within their traditional art forms, however, only minimal influence of foreign societies is evident in Black Africa, although certain symbols and motifs, such as the 'eternal' figure-of-eight knot which derives from the Moslem Fulani tribes, have filtered south deep into the Congo and have been adopted by African tribes (*plate 31*). With regard to their sculpture, the forms remain strictly traditional, conforming to a well-established iconography.

African art is perhaps best understood as being a flexible classicism in which great scope exists for individual expression on the part of the artist. The sophistication which marks one piece as superior to another comes through individual interpretation on the part of the artist who, whilst working within the convention stipulated by tradition, still has sufficient freedom to create a work of striking individuality. Although displaying many signs of uniqueness, a work will still retain the traditional motifs, representations and references which enable it to convey its symbolism through a language employed by artists of the tribe and understood by its members.

Tribality is the essence of African art and each tribal group is a highly autonomous structure. Stylistic forms of expression within traditional African society have been greatly divided by tribal boundaries, with little of the cross-flow of styles common in Western art. As an extension of this, it has been observed that whilst there is no concept of individual portraiture, every mask is true to a tribal facial type.

Even in those few masks in which a degree of portraiture is intended, the equal emphasis normally given to all the individual features by the artist tends to obscure personal identity. This feature of African masks is as apparent in the refined Mannerist masks of the Baule, Guro and Dan from the Liberian/Ivory Coast region as it is in the Expressionist masks from the Yoruba of Nigeria and the tribes of the Cameroon Grasslands. Both the idealized faces and the equal emphasis on component forms give expression to traditionally desirable qualities such as wisdom, strength, youth and vitality.

Within African art, the aspect of the face has strict iconographic meaning. Both masks and figures are reliquaries of divine power, whether their function is intended to be profound, or frivolous and entertaining. As such they are consecrated and imbued with power by the priests and their associated secret societies and conform to strict iconographic canons. Amongst the various tribes, vastly different means may be employed to represent the same concepts, ideals or emotions. Within the Yaure (*plates 16, 17*), Guro (*plate 14*), Dan (*plate 11*) and Bachokwe (*plate 35*) tribes for example, a forward-gazing posture, combined with slit eyes and a frozen facial expression, may be used to indicate a state of spiritual possession. The same state is portrayed in the Yoruba and Cameroon Grasslands tribes by the use of boldly protruding facial features, especially the eyes, combined with a backward inclination of the head.

Several forms and motifs have become conventionalized and hold established meanings understood by a wide range of tribes scattered over large areas. A high domed forehead is generally a sign of wisdom and unmarred spirituality whilst the use of white pigmentation, as on the Ibo maiden mask (*plate 22*), indicates ghosts, the spirits of the dead and an 'otherworldly' quality. In many parts of Africa, the buffalo or bush-cow is considered to be the familiar of witches. Masks taking this form, as well as those derived from other horned animals, especially antelopes, are used in ceremonies connected with exorcism, spirit transmigration, the invocation of natural power through witchcraft and the honouring of the ancestors (*plate 10*).

Masks become reliquaries of divine power and must therefore be either as beautiful or as terrifying as possible in order for the spirit to choose to inhabit them. They are generally worn together with an accompanying regalia of bark cloths, fibre fringes, animal fur and a variety of attachments including cowrie shells, sections of animal horn and miscellaneous metal suspensions. The dancer, when wearing the mask and accompanying regalia in the prescribed manner, is invested with the spirit of the mask and is effectively no longer human. The spirit of the mask will cause the dancer to carry himself with the gait of one possessed and speak with an altered voice, often caused by a voice disguiser, which normally consists of a hollow tube, one end of which is partially covered by a membrane.

The role of the carver within the tribe is primarily decided by the ethnic group to which his tribe belongs. Amongst the agrarian Bantu and Bantoid peoples of West Africa, the artist may be engaged for only a small percentage of his time in the actual process of carving. Generally, he will remain a farmer and will have to contribute his share of work in the fields, with the time allocated to carving being strictly limited or confined solely to his leisure time. Occasionally, however, an artist may become so renowned that he is able to devote his time solely to carving with a large retinue of apprentice carvers working under him.

Amongst the peoples of the West Sudan, the position of the carver is very different. As a Moslem religious group, these tribes attempt as far as possible to refrain from manual work, the task of manufacturing masks and images being left to the lowly caste of smiths. The smiths, on the one hand scorned and rejected, are also treated with a degree of deference and respect as no one wishes to incur the displeasure of the spirit world with which the smiths are in liaison. Famous smiths may even command positions of power and respect, and are in some tribes, notably the Dogon, viewed as the progenitors of civilization.

Within the Bantu and Bantoid peoples, the manufacture of high-quality works is well rewarded, often in what seems an excessively generous manner for the amount of the carver's time employed. Renowned professional carvers may be rewarded for their labours through the exchange of livestock, with as many as three goats being traded for a single high-quality mask. In Cameroon, tradition dictates that in exchange for a powerful and inspiring mask a carver should receive a girl suitable either for work in the fields or for marriage. Even the non-professional farmer/carver receives food and produce as recompense for time lost from his labours in the fields. Through their role as the 'powerful masters of fire' in alliance with the occult, the smiths often rise to high positions within the tribe, coming to prominence in the role of priest, adviser to the king, or leader of one of the secret societies.

It is widely accepted that the finest African works of art have been produced within a traditional tribal context, for use by members of the tribe. It is of paramount importance that the smith be fully cognisant with and totally immersed in the customs and images of his society. Unlike many Western artists, the traditional African artist is never in opposition to his society and peer group, as the forms he uses reflect those considered the most traditionally perfect and desirable. His is a devotional art in which religious representation remains the essence of the work. It is for this reason that the carvings produced by tribes in which the old religious and cultural values are breaking down appear decadent and lacking in refinement. It is also for this reason that traditional pieces of fine quality command such high prices when offered to institutions and collectors.

The main purpose behind the carving of masks is the desire to give a real and tangible form to the spirit world, as a means of gaining some control over the universal creative force. This force is seen as present in every living thing and capable of being used in a positive and protective manner. The accruing of credit in the spiritual world is considered a real and necessary aspect of life.

Responsibility for the control, understanding and operation of the ritual cults associated with the vital life force falls upon one member of the tribe, the priest or 'witch-doctor', as he has become known in Western society. The priest maintained a powerful position and was expected to predict and control the acts of beneficent and malevolent spirits, and to know the plants and minerals useful in the treatment of illness. A careful guard was kept to ensure that the tradition so important in the welfare of the tribe was preserved.

To assist the priest, there existed secret societies of specially initiated men. These societies were also responsible for the safeguarding of authority, the maintenance of obedience and the preservation of tradition. Through these societies, young men were taught the essentials in the battle to survive as well as being vested with an understanding of and respect for the spirit world.

Masks were used in many different capacities including initiation ceremonies, cult rituals of the priests, the passage of men from one grade to another, the celebration of harvest, the judgement of prisoners, the exorcism of evil spirits, and even entertainment, when the wearer would act as a buffoon whilst not wholly divorcing himself from elements of the spirit world. They assume a vast variety of different forms according to their intended function. The 'Mother' masks of the Dan (*plate 11*) represent an ideal of female beauty. According to Himmelheber, it is important that these masks, used in initiation ceremonies, should not frighten the children, for it is through them that they will learn their tradition.

Generally, we can to some extent ascertain function through the form of the mask. There is, however, no absolutely reliable clue to be gained from appearance alone, for the function may be radically altered by the addition of a variety of magical substances.

As an extension of this, it must be remembered that for every rule there is an exception and this is certainly the case with African art. Rules change overnight with the development of the tribe, and art forms change with them. For this reason, it is wise to preface every belief which we hold about African societies and art forms with 'perhaps'. The structure of the tribe and the nature of its religious convictions are changing rapidly, and through these changes new art forms emerge as a living reflection of contemporary society. These contrast sharply with pieces produced for the tourist trade which, whilst sometimes carved in the traditional style, lack life and vitality, the understanding of and reasons for their forms having been long forgotten.

A map at the end of the book shows the location of the tribes mentioned in the text.

1. *Dogon mask*

Wood with black crusty patination. 17in (43·2cm)

The Dogon tribe inhabit the northern region of Mali and would appear to have been forced to take refuge in the arid and mountainous Bandiagara Escarpment under pressure from the large kingdom of Mossi some time between the twelfth and fourteenth centuries. Carbon-14 tests on carvings found in caves lend support to these dates although the Dogon themselves, while treating the carvings with great reverence, claim that they are the work of a previous population, the Tellem, rather than of their own ancestors.

This mask is thought to come from the Samane people who live at the bottom of the Bandiagara Escarpment and who, although they mix with the Dogon, have their own masks. The style of this mask is, however, indistinguishable from that of the true Dogon ones. Known as *ibi bongo*, it represents hunters and combines a variety of human and animal attributes, the masterly balancing of forms giving it great presence and power.

Private Collection

2. *Dogon mask*

Wood with painted decoration. 50in (127cm)

This mask, which may now be provisionally attributed to the Dogon tribe, is of a type still attributed by many people to the Mossi or Bobo. It has been suggested that this type of mask represents a rabbit, the gently curving superstructure being its ears. Carved in soft wood, the sensitive curve of the 'ears' and their gradual thickening to form the ridge-like nose, together with the precise red and black geometric decoration, speak of a strong appreciation of pattern and form.

Private Collection

3. *Bambara antelope mask*

Wood. 16¼in (41·25cm)

The Bambara are one of the largest tribes living in Mali, numbering about one million. The culture has been strongly Islamic since the seventeenth century and remains so today with the city of Bamako serving as the centre of religion, trade and commerce. The most powerful Bambara society is the *Komo* which has a smith as its leader. The smiths form an elite group known as the *Numu* and, together with the *Kule*, another caste of carvers who form a distinct sub-group, they are responsible for the production of all masks and figures for the Bambara. Craftsmen from these two castes travel freely amongst the Bambara and may therefore work in a variety of different styles while still retaining the traditional elements integral to each area.

This mask belongs to a group of animal masks associated with the *Kore* society and represents an antelope. The kapok wood from which it has been carved has been blackened with red-hot iron and then polished with shea butter. Masks from this society are used to call upon the water spirit to provide rain, the ceremony taking place every seven years or during any particularly dry period.

London, Collection Josef Herman

4. *Igbira mask*

Wood with seeds and beeswax. 21in (53·5cm)

This mask bears a powerful combination of human and animal (possibly antelope) attributes and probably comes from the Igbira tribe who live near the confluence of the Niger and Benue Rivers. Although masks like this are found in a number of West African tribes, the decorative use of red abrus seeds is especially characteristic of the Igbira. The surface of the mask is eroded and sections of the blackened beeswax are missing, but enough remains to show the dramatic way in which the angular qualities of the mask have been accentuated by the geometric fragmentation of the surface.

New York, Private Collection

5. *Mossi mask*

Wood. 66in (168cm)

The Mossi people of Upper Volta are comprised of two separate branches, the Mossi-Yatenga and the Mossi-Wagadugu. Both are subject to the rule of King Moro-Naba who, from his capital at Wagadugu, continues a tradition of sacral kingship which has its roots in the golden age from the eleventh to the fifteenth century. The Mossi people share many traits with other tribes of the West Sudan in spite of their Islamic tradition, which does, however, prohibit the manufacture of portrait masks; the faces of masks such as this, therefore, bear only a vague resemblance to human form. The abstract oval of this mask represents a spirit face and has stylized attributes of both human and animal forms. Masks such as this are cared for by the *Wango* men's society and women are forbidden to look at them. They are used in a protective capacity at funerals and other ritual occasions and remain the property of the 'Lord of the soil'.

London, Museum of Mankind

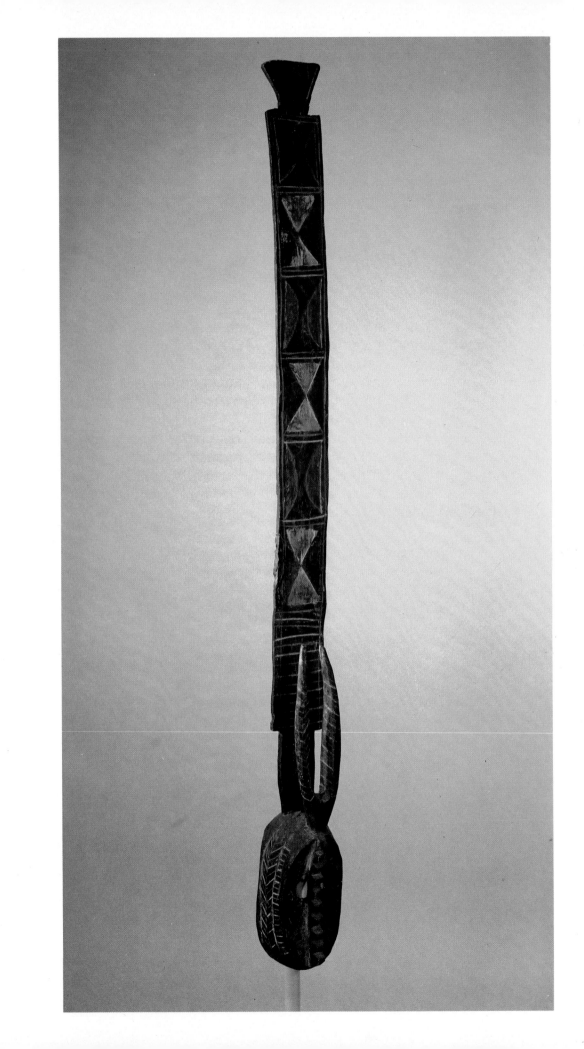

6. *Bobo mask*

Wood. 27¼in (69cm)

This mask belongs to a branch of the Bobo known as the Bobo-Fing or Black Bobo who live mainly in the region north of Bobo Diulasso and south of Nuna. In contrast to the strongly geometric two-dimensional masks of their counterparts, the Bobo-Ule or Red Bobo, those of the Bobo-Fing are decidedly three-dimensional. They are generally painted and often decorated with red jequirity seeds. Many masks of this type represent animals, commonly rams or buffalo. This example, in the form of a human face, is unusual in that it is surmounted by a human figure; the majority bear a geometric superstructure.

London, Museum of Mankind

7. *Gurunsi mask*

Wood with pigment. 27½in (70cm)

The Gurunsi border the Bobo and produce the tall board-like masks which are also used by the Bobo and the Nuna. These masks are carved in lightweight wood, and sometimes exceed three metres in height. They are intended to be viewed from the front and rely for their impact on decorative geometric patterns, which are said to be heraldic emblems. Tall masks such as this example are believed to be female and are used in farming rituals. Worn in pairs, they are used on only one night of the year, in December. The dancers leap and genuflect before the whole village.

London, Museum of Mankind

8. Baga mask

Wood. 47½in (122cm)

The Baga is one of the three main tribes of south-western Guinea, the others being the Nalu and the Landuma. Because of the great intermingling between them, they are often treated as a single group. This mask belongs to the most impressive class of cult objects made by the dominant *Simo* secret society and represents *Nimba*, the goddess of fertility. It conforms closely to the iconographic conventions, with the individual elements combining to give an abstract stylized form of immense visual impact. Unlike many masks now removed from their tribal context, this one has the thick raffia fringe which would have concealed the wearer and so added greatly to its otherworldly quality. It would have been used in rituals to generate fertility in either a woman, a rice field or a palm grove, and was also believed to give protection to pregnant women.

London, Museum of Mankind

9. *Bassa mask*

Wood. 11in (28cm)

The Bassa are one of a large group of Dan-Ngere sub-tribes whose work has many similarities with the classical northern Dan style of idealized naturalism. This mask contains many features of the classic Dan masks but at the same time has an expressionist quality found only amongst the Dan sub-tribes.

London, Collection Josef Herman

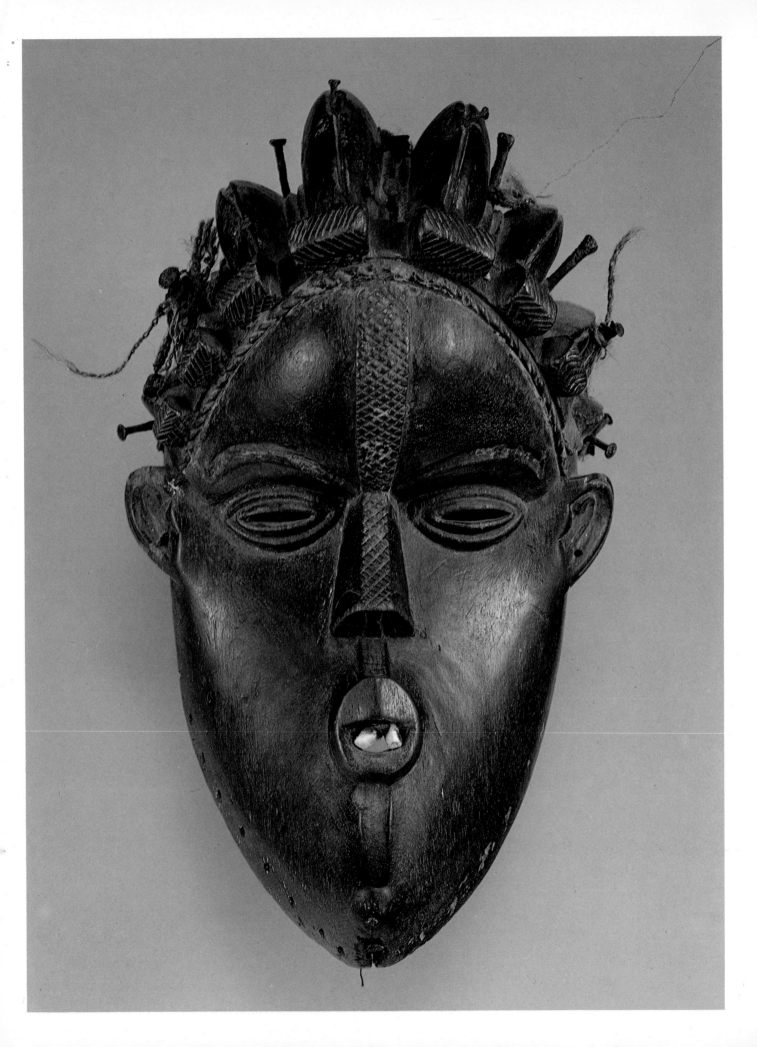

10. *Dan mask*

Wood with buffalo horns and traces of red ochre. 15¾in (40cm)

The name Dan is a general term used to encompass a
large number of Mande-speaking sub-tribes in the region
of east Liberia, the west Ivory Coast and southern Guinea.
This mask, representing a bush-cow, comes from the
village of Douékoué, near Toulepleu, on the border
between the northern Ivory Coast and Liberia. The buffalo
or bush-cow is considered one of the most powerful
animals of the wild and, in many parts of Africa, is viewed
as the familiar of witches. Although one cannot be certain
about its function, it is likely that the wearer used the
mask to invoke the power of the bush-cow.

New York, Private Collection

11. *Dan mask*

Wood and fibre. 9¾in (24·8cm)

Dan masks normally have a strong naturalistic quality which makes them among the most accessible of African masks. This quality has also helped to ensure their continuing popularity with collectors. The Dan are prolific manufacturers of masks; different types are carved to cover practically all aspects of life, the most important masks being those which, representing the powerful bush-spirit, are made to act as judges and law-makers for the tribe. This example is of a far more representative type than the preceding one; known as *Tangkag-le*, it is worn in public performances to dance and act out pantomimes. It is likely that the headdress on this mask has been transferred to it from another one.

Private Collection

12. *Bete mask*

Wood with copper nails. 11½in (29·25cm)

The Bete share many religious, social and artistic conventions with the Dan, while remaining an entirely separate tribe. This mask embodies a wart-hog or bush-demon. The parallel ridges would appear to be a stylized representation of the inward-curving tusks of the wart-hog and are a splendid example of the highly cubistic treatment of form found among some Dan-Ngere tribes.

London, Collection Josef Herman

13. *Ngere mask*

Wood. 11in (28cm)

This mask is of the *kao gle* (bush-spirit) type and belongs to another sub-tribe of the Dan-Ngere complex. The *kao gle* fulfils a number of different functions, one of the main ones being to attack unpredictably a member of the tribe or his property. The belief behind this is that the *kao gle* serves to test the fidelity of the people towards their ruler; those who truly love him will not take offence at the wrong done them.

London, Collection Josef Herman

14. *Guro mask*

Wood. 12in (30·5cm)

The Guro of the Central Ivory Coast, an ancient Mande-speaking people, are one of the indigenous tribes of the area who were forced to retreat into the jungles by the invasion from Ghana of the Baule tribe with their Ashanti rulers, around the middle of the eighteenth century. The masks and figures of the Guro display a poetical refinement which has made them highly sought-after by collectors and has given inspiration to many artists. It takes little imagination to see the parallels between this mask and many of Modigliani's portrait heads.

London, Collection Dr Werner Muensterberger

15. *Guro mask*

Wood with pigment. 25in (63·5cm)

This mask, particularly rare in its large size and fine quality, displays many of the beautiful features which have made Guro masks especially sought by collectors.

The rounded forms and carefully proportioned flowing features combine to produce an effect of almost otherworldly beauty. The coiffure is carefully constructed and, like many Guro masks, is surmounted by a wooden horn. The function of the mask is uncertain, although it has been suggested that it is associated with a cult of fertility.

Private Collection

16. *Yaure mask*

Wood. 23¼in (59cm)

This mask, formerly in the collection of the sculptor Sir Jacob Epstein, clearly shows the refined treatment of form and the restrained sense of beauty that are found in the art of the Baule and their sub-tribes. This mask was carved by the Yaure sub-tribe, and, although somewhat angular in appearance, it contains many of the decorative elements of the Classical Baule tradition. The Baule and their sub-tribes are amongst the most prolific carvers in Africa; every house has in it a personal ancestor figure and many masks, such as this one, were made for pleasure rather than for religious purposes.

London, Museum of Mankind

17. *Yaure mask*

Wood. 7½in (19cm)

The Yaure are one of the numerous Baule sub-tribes of the central Ivory Coast and their sculpture is clearly influenced by that of the Guro, one of the indigenous tribes of the region.

Like the Baule, they carve in hard, dense woods which lend themselves to the characteristic fine detailing and sensitive modelling impossible to reproduce in softer woods. After completion of the carving process, the wood is soaked in mud or in the juice of a variety of berries, which imparts a dark glossy patina.

This mask is probably a representation of the sun; the form is almost two-dimensional and is designed to have greatest impact when viewed from the front. The serrated border is typical of Yaure masks and is derived from the Guro style.

New York, Private Collection

18. *Yoruba mask*

Wood with traces of red pigment. 15in (38cm)

The Yoruba people number more than twelve million and are the largest tribe in West Africa. From early times, they have occupied an extensive area in south-west Nigeria, Dahomey and Togo. At one time peasant farmers, they have, over the past few centuries, formed themselves into city states. Oyo, the biggest of these, became so powerful at the turn of the seventeenth century that even the states of Ife, Benin and Dahomey paid tribute to it.

Within the Yoruba religion, there exists a complex pantheon of mythological beings. The principal deity is *Olorun*, the creator of the universe; his messengers, the *Orisha*, are deified beings who often embody natural phenomena such as thunder.

This mask, made to be worn on top of the head, probably portrays the *Orisha Eshu*, a trickster who acts as a foil to *Ifa*, the guardian of order. The faces display clearly recognizable Yoruba features; a typical ridged coiffure is apparent on the main head, the features protrude and tribal scarifications are clearly visible on the cheeks and forehead.

London, Collection Lance Entwistle

19. *Benin belt mask*

Ivory. 9⅗in (24·5cm)

This mask, dating from the reign of the Oba Esigie in the
early sixteenth century, is one of a handful of similar
masks which were collected by a British punitive
expedition in 1897 and were found together in a trunk in
the bedroom of the Oba Avonrame. Portraying an Oba in
ceremonial dress, it was intended to be worn as a belt mask
and is one of the finest West African ivory carvings. Like
the bronze altar heads of the same period, this mask was
not intended to be a portrait but rather a stereotype of
royalty. It shows a sensitivity of modelling unequalled in
later pieces, which relied heavily upon the classic style of
sixteenth-century works for their inspiration.

London, Museum of Mankind

20. *Benin hip mask*

Bronze with copper inlay. 8in (20cm)

The first contact between Benin and Europe came when the Portuguese traveller J. A. d'Alveiro visited the city of Benin in 1485. In his reports he wrote enthusiastically of the splendour of the Oba's palace, which comprised elaborate mud-brick buildings, the wood columns of which were decorated with bronze plaques commemorating the Oba's victories. Equally astonishing was the existence of a sophisticated imperial system which enabled the Oba to rule efficiently and with absolute authority.

This mask, designed for wear on the hip, portrays a ram's head with a border of nine mud-fish encircling the broad, ridged collar. It is likely that this piece is the work of Owo craftsmen working in Benin, as the sensitivity and subtlety of the modelling surpass the best of Benin animal sculpture. Certain stylistic features such as the accomplished craftsmanship of the copper insets indicate that the piece was made in the sixteenth century.

London, Collection Lance Entwistle

21. *Ibo male mask*

Wood with traces of pigment. 11¾in (27·25cm)

The Ibo extend across the main region of eastern Nigeria and, after the Yoruba, form the second largest tribal group in West Africa. They comprise a large number of sub-tribes, but, unlike the Yoruba, they have resisted centralization and have no large towns.

Drawing influence from many of the surrounding tribes, carvings amongst the Ibo show a great diversity of style and are often difficult to ascribe to any one sub-tribe. This mask represents a male figure and belongs to the large group of masks intended for use in the masked plays, funeral rites, initiation and fertility ceremonies of the numerous traditional Ibo secret societies.

London, Collection Josef Herman

22. *Ibo maiden mask*

Wood with black and white pigments. 15¾in (43cm)

This mask belongs to the *mmwo* men's secret society and represents dead young wives. Appearing only once every three years, it was used in ceremonies connected with the initiation of young boys. The face is whitened with kaolin in the manner employed by a number of other tribes, notably the Ashira-Bapunu; in almost every case, this was done to portray an aspect of the spirit world.

London, Museum of Mankind

23. *Ibibio mask*

Wood with rich encrusted patination. 13in (33cm)

To the south-east of the Ibo are found the Ibibio.
Although, like the Ibo, they have never formed large
urban groups, the influence of the *Ekpo* society pervades
every village. Boldly visual masks, such as this one, are
used by the *Ekpo* to instil a sense of terror and fear in the
uninitiated. Often, their masks contain a grotesque and
disturbing exaggerated realism. The disfiguring effects of
diseases such as palsy often serve to inspire their forms.

London, Collection Lance Entwistle

24. *Ekoi mask*

Wood with hide covering. 16¼in (41cm)

It is thought that the extremely naturalistic style of the
Ekoi group of tribes may derive from a practice of tying the
severed heads of their enemies above their own heads in
the belief that the blood would enrich the fertility of the
fields. As recently as the nineteenth century, they are
reputed to have used the skin of slaves to stretch over the
carved wooden frames of masks. More recently, the skin of
goats and antelopes has been used. Often, as with this
example, great pains are taken to produce a realistic effect.
Cane insets represent the teeth, metal insets embellish the
eyes, the skin is pigmented, and painted tribal scarification
markings indicate the rank of the owner.

London, Museum of Mankind

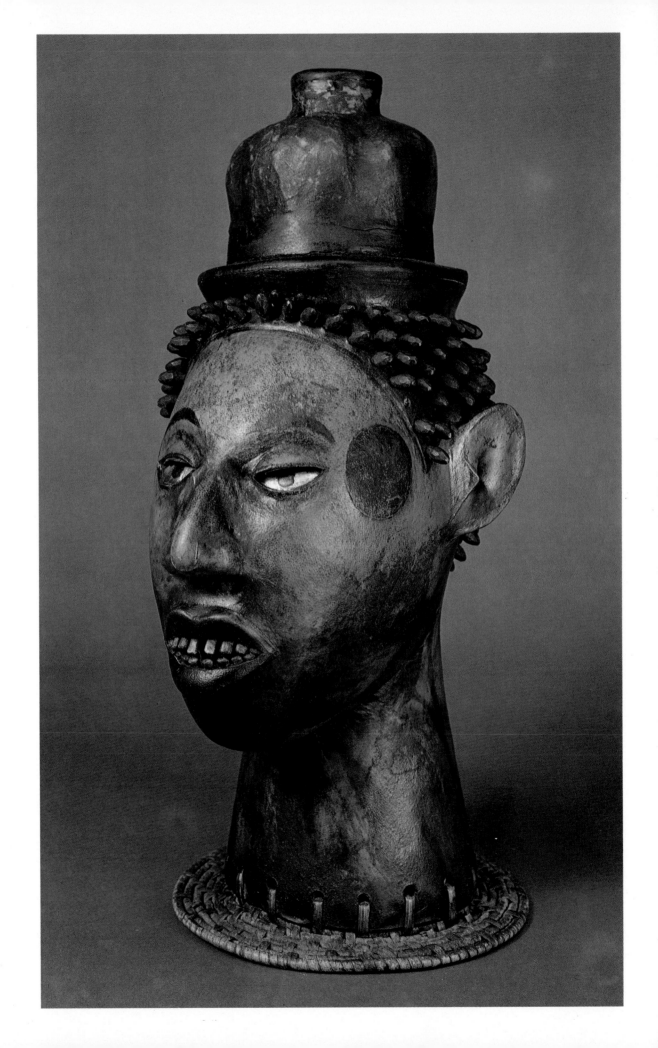

25. *Cameroons mask*

Wood with encrusted pigmentation. 13in (33cm)

This mask probably comes from the Bangangte in the western part of the Cameroons Grasslands, one of the numerous sub-tribes of the extensive Bamileke group. Absolute identification is, however, difficult as a great mixing of styles occurs between the prosperous and hierarchical village states.

The masks of the Cameroons were intended to be worn on top of the head and did not therefore require eye-holes. They were generally carved for kings and in return the carver was handsomely rewarded. As 'royal art', it is thought that they represented kings, the swollen features common among them intended to convey the well-nourished state made possible by royal affluence.

London, Collection Lance Entwistle

26. *Fang mask*

Wood with white pigmentation. 10in (25·5cm)

The Fang tribe, famous for the great refinement of their figure sculpture, also produce sensitively proportioned masks such as this.

Within Fang society masks play a smaller role than in many other tribes. They are mainly used to exorcise spirits and in the enforcement of law through the *Ngi* society.

Unlike Fang sculpture, the masks display an austere simplicity of form. The use of black to highlight the fine features, apparent in this example, is typical.

London, Museum of Mankind

27. *Fang helmet mask*

Wood with traces of pigment. 15in (38cm)

All four faces carved on this mask display similar features to those found on the single white-faced masks of the Fang. The geometric fragmentation of the surface is, however, untypical of Fang masks and gives a vivid demonstration of the diversity found in the sculpture of this large tribe.

London, Museum of Mankind

28. *Mahongwe mask*

Wood. 15¾in (40cm)

The Mahongwe of Congo-Brazzaville are chiefly known for their brass-covered reliquary figures, which were supposed to guard the bones of ancestors. This mask belongs to a group about which relatively little is known although the style is reminiscent of masks from the Fang and Bakwele tribes who inhabit the same area.

New York, Private Collection

29. *Ashira-Bapunu mask*

Wood with white, red-brown and black pigmentation. 13in (33cm)

White-faced masks of this type are produced by many of the tribes of the southern Gabon region, but perhaps the most beautiful of these come from the Ashira-Bapunu group of Congo-Brazzaville. This mask is typical of the naturalistic sculpture of the Bapunu, and is strongly reminiscent of Japanese masks. The markings on the face are extremely rare and definite attribution is difficult. Another iconographically indistinguishable mask was collected by the Swedish missionary Ephraim Andersson in the Bakota village of N'Tima and it has been suggested that this example may in fact have been carved by the Bakota who border the Bapunu to the north.

Private Collection

30. *Bakongo mask*

Wood with pigment. 10in (25·5cm)

The tribes of the Lower Congo, living along the banks of the mouth of the Congo River, were among the first traditional African tribes to have any prolonged contact with Europeans. For two hundred years Portuguese missionaries lived with and succeeded in converting many of the tribes of this region before finally succumbing to an upsurge of popular indigenous belief in the early eighteenth century.

This mask, probably from the Mayombe tribe, is one of the very few produced by the Bakongo tribes. Little research has been done into the use of these masks, but it is probable that this example represents a woman from a noble family. The low cap is derived from woven raffia caps worn by the Bakongo women which are almost always found on maternity figures.

London, Collection Lance Entwistle

31. *Bena Biombo mask*

Wood. 20½in (50cm)

The Bena Biombo, living between the Kasai and Lulua rivers, belong to a group of tribes much influenced by the powerful Bakuba.

Elements such as the zone of black and white incised decoration on the forehead are recognizable derivations from the Bakuba masks from the north and those of the Bapende across the Kasai river. The Bena Biombo are, however, an entirely different group from the Bakuba, with stylistic forms drawn from a variety of sources, the 'eternal knot' on the chin deriving from Fulani Moslem influence. This large vigorous mask, with its boldly carved features, belongs to the best-known type of Bena Biombo carvings. Worn as a helmet, it was apparently used for entertainment.

London, Collection Josef Herman

32. *Basuku mask*

Wood. 17in (43cm)

For a long time the Basuku were classed as being part of
the larger Bayaka tribe with no independent art forms of
their own. A closer examination has, however, revealed a
distinct style, more refined and less expressionist than that
of the Bayaka. This mask is typical in that it is carved in
the form of a helmet and is surmounted by a three-
dimensional superstructure in the form of an animal. The
white pigmentation is thought to signify the spirit realm
out of which young male initiates are supposed to be
reborn as men ready for marriage.

London, Museum of Mankind

33. *Bakuba mask*

Wood. 9½in (24cm)

The masks of the ancient central Congo kingdom of
Bakuba are among the most imaginative and colourful in
all Africa. Although some Bakuba masks are supposed to
act as law enforcers, the majority reflect the demands of
popular art. The vivid geometric patterns of this mask are
reminiscent of those of *musese*, the beautiful Bakuba cloth
which is woven and layer-cut in the manner of plush
velvet. To enable the wearer to see, the protruding eyes
are pierced around the perimeter in imitation of the eyes
of a chameleon.

London, Museum of Mankind

34. *Bachokwe mask*

Wood and fibre. 11in (28cm)

This mask, representing a chief and symbolizing wealth, comes from the Lunda-Bachokwe tribe of the southern Congo. Known as *chikungu*, these masks were originally only worn by the sons of chiefs at *makishi* initiation dances, the enthronement of kings and in fertility rites. The semi-circular ridge projecting from the chin represents a beard, and a large curving headdress known as *chihongo*, a symbol of royalty, would have originally been attached to the fibre coiffure.

Over the past century the original function of these masks has become obscured, with the ritual use declining in importance. They have been used in displays of wealth and status on the part of the chief and even just to entertain European visitors. Naturally, as the ritual significance of the masks has decreased, so too has the quality, and fine old examples such as this have become increasingly rare.

London, Collection Lance Entwistle

35. *Bachokwe mask*

Wood and fibre with brass studs. 10in (25·5cm)

This mask, known as *mwana pwo*, is the female counterpart to the mask on the preceding page and is used in conjunction with it in the *pwo* fertility dance. The mask represents a young woman freshly emerged from the initiation schools in the bush and ready for marriage. Like other Bachokwe sculpture, the form is fleshy and substantial, combining dignity and force to produce an image of deified humanity. It is said that frozen facial expressions, such as that on this mask, are used to portray a revered state of quietude, which is supposed to attest to a harmonious relationship between the individual and the vital force of the universe.

London, Collection Lance Entwistle

36. *Bapende mask*

Wood and fibre. 18in (46cm)

This mask, belonging to a type known as *mbuya*, is typical of the style of the Katundu chiefdom among the central and western Bapende. Worn by the celebrants at coming out parties of newly initiated young men who have just been circumcised, these masks, according to William Fagg, represent revered mythological beings and ancestors such as chiefs and their wives, hunters, prophets and sages.

London, Collection Lance Entwistle

37. *Balega mask*

Wood with pigment and fibre. 8in (20·3cm)

The Balega, formerly known as the Warega, live to the north-west of Lake Tanganyika and dwell in small villages with no central structure of authority. Their social life is dominated by the *Bwami* society to which every man and woman belongs. This society is divided into five grades for men and three for women, the art of the Balega being produced to signify the passage of members from one grade to another.

Carved in hardwood and decorated with kaolin and a banana fibre beard, this mask probably belongs to a type classified by Daniel Biebuyck as *Nenekisi*, meaning 'master of the land'. Like most Balega masks, this example is not made for wear on the face, but is normally worn on the arm or carried in a 'power basket'.

Private Collection

38. *Batetela mask*

Wood, fur and fibre. 16½in (42cm)

The masks of the Batetela, which depend for their impact upon bold incised linear patterns and cubistic forms, are similar to those of the Basonge who live further to the south.

    This mask was collected over seventy years ago by the Hungarian adventurer and collector Emile Torday. According to Torday, the mask was worn by a *wichi*, or practitioner of white magic, and was used to frighten crowds.

London, Museum of Mankind

39. *Baluba mask*

Wood. 14⅝in (37cm)

The Baluba form the largest culturally integrated tribal group in the Congo. This mask characterizes many facets of Baluba carving; the smooth vaulted forehead, small protruding mouth, 'coffee-bean' eyes and small cat-like ears combine to produce a rounded and fleshy effect. Like all Baluba carvings, the surface of this mask has been carefully blackened and polished by the carver and its subsequent owners.

Private Collection

40. *Makonde helmet mask*

Wood. 12in (30·5cm)

The Makonde are the most accomplished carvers in
eastern Africa. They are best known in recent years for
their grotesque and sinuous figure groups carved in ebony,
but the traditional Makonde smith worked in a highly
naturalistic manner, producing helmet masks and, more
rarely, standing figures. This mask, although probably
unique in that it depicts an Arab trader, is carved in the
traditional style; human hair has been used to further its
realistic effect.

London, Museum of Mankind

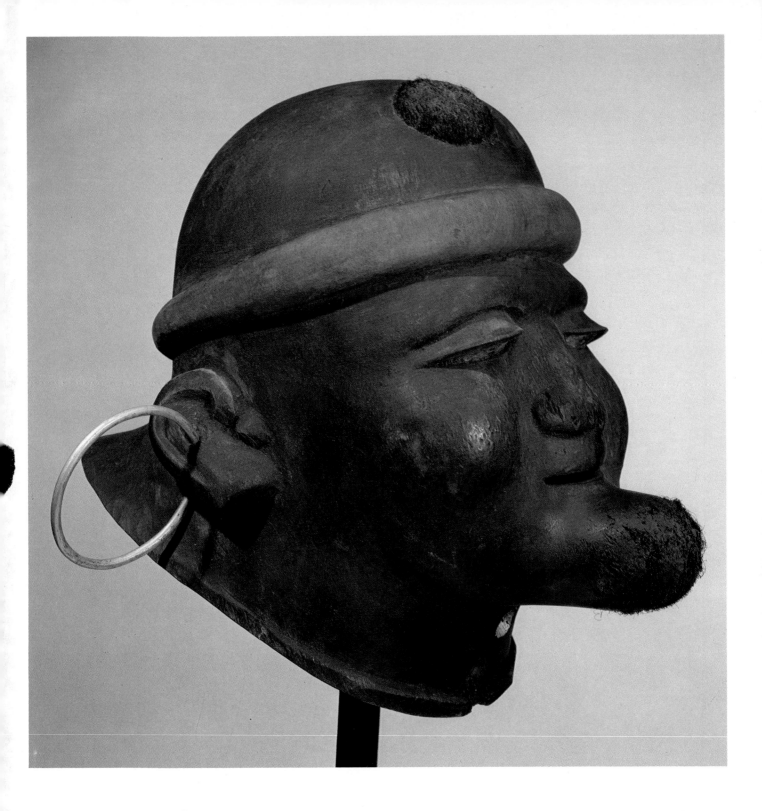

Map of Africa showing the location of the tribes mentioned in this book

1 Dogon
2 Bambara
3 Mossi
4 Gurunsi
5 Bobo
6 Baga
7 Bassa
8 Dan
9 Bete
10 Ngere
11 Guro
12 Yaure
13 Yoruba
14 Igbira
15 Benin
16 Ibo
17 Ibibio
18 Ekoi
19 Cameroons
20 Fang
21 Mahongwe
22 Ashira Bapunu
23 Bakongo
24 Bena Biombo
25 Basuku
26 Bakuba
27 Bapende
28 Bachokwe
29 Balega
30 Batetela
31 Baluba
32 Makonde